5 *Short Topics in*
System Administration

W9-CSX-160

Edited by William LeFebvre

Hiring System Administrators

By Gretchen Phillips

Published by the USENIX Association for
SAGE, the System Administrators Guild
1999

Copies of these publications are available to members of SAGE for
$10.00 and to non-members for $12.00. Outside the US and Canada,
please add $3.50 per copy for postage (via printed matter).

For copies and for membership information, please contact:

The USENIX Association
2560 Ninth Street, Suite 215
Berkeley, CA 94710 USA
Email: *office@usenix.org*
Web: *http://www.usenix.org*

First Printing 1999

Contents

 **Foreword**

My second full-time job out of college placed me in charge of a systems support group for an entire department. I was given the position because of my strength in systems management. I soon discovered that the job entailed more than working with computers: it also required managing people. I was unexpectedly faced with the task of molding disparate personalities into a successful team.

The single aspect of that job that I dreaded most was hiring new people. I pored over piles of resumes without knowing how to separate the wheat from the chaff. I interviewed candidates without any idea of what to ask or how to judge the responses.

Many books have been written explaining how one can be effective as an interviewee. This publication views the problem from the other side of the desk. Designed for the reluctant manager, it will help to organize a team's objectives and develop an effective hiring strategy. With its focus on the systems administration profession, it will, I am sure, be an important addition to your library.

William LeFebvre
Alpharetta, GA
March 1999

Acknowledgments

The development of any written work is a nontrivial process. This booklet came about because many people were willing to talk, listen, answer questions, read, and be supportive.

It is my privilege to acknowledge the input and support from many people in the development of this booklet. The SAGE community willingly provided input on hiring techniques; those that read draft copies provided enlightening comments on things that had been omitted or overlooked and provided encouraging support that led to the final product. My family and coworkers were understanding during the entire process. In particular, sincere thanks are due to John D. Armstrong, Charles F. Dunn, Paul Evans, Stan Heller, Paul R. Joslin, Rob Kolstad, Kristin M. Kuntz, John S. Quarterman, Peter Salus, John Sechrest, and Pat Wilson for their particular contributions to this adventure. Finally, thank you to Maggie Taylor who worked many hours to help me craft a better booklet.

I hope that this booklet is a tool that is useful for others in the selection of system administrators.

1.0 Introduction

Technology continuously grows and changes and now permeates every area of society. The development and support of new technologies is dependent on both the developers and the support infrastructure individuals, commonly given the title of System Administrator. System administrators can be obtained in a variety of ways, including (re)training existing staff, hiring experienced individuals, or hiring inexperienced and trainable individuals. No matter which road is chosen in filling positions, the process used is important; future successes are often based on the hiring choices made.

Hiring procedures vary widely, depending on the local environments and types of organizations. Some are formal with a wide range of rules and regulations. Some are less formal but expect the same outcome.

Choosing and using a process that is right for your organization makes a difference in the overall quality of the team. A poor selection process can result in an employee who does not fit with the organizational culture, the project group or team, or the supervisor. Taking time to use a thoughtful and complete selection process can save time and effort as well as disappointment in the long term. A process kind to both applicants and the interview team can build relationships that outlast the interview process and provide fertile ground for future hiring opportunities.

1.1 The Hiring Process

The hiring process is a flexible mechanism that can be used to build or change the composition of a team, project, group, or organization as a whole. This is particularly true in smaller organizations, where the addition or departure of a single staff member can result in a dramatic difference. Additions made to strength areas can give a group added depth. Additions made to underdeveloped areas can give a group new breadth. Hiring a new personality type can bring a new dynamic to a group; hiring someone who fits in like an long-lost companion can add to the existing compatibility of a group. While at the outset it is not possible to know what similarities or differences the applicant pool will provide, it is important to be aware of this dynamic in the evaluation of each candidate.

The hiring process can be a potential employee's first view of your organization. To help your organization make a good first impression, consider the following questions:

- What does the interview process say about your organization to potential candidates?
- Do the applicants feel they are wanted?
- Are they excited about the possibility of working in an organization that has a hiring process such as the one that your organization uses?
- Is the process simple, complicated, scary, or a challenge?

Providing a positive interview experience to each applicant can enrich the reputation of your organization and potentially develop opportunities for attracting excellent candidates for future positions.

1.2 Overview of Important Issues

A variety of issues need to be considered before the hiring process begins in earnest. These include:

- The number of people being hired at a time
- The size of the existing team
- The strengths and weaknesses of the current staff
- The current (and future) mission of the team
- The current (and future) projects of the team

Each of these issues will have an impact on the individual who is considered for the position. A large existing staff can afford more flexibility in the type of individual hired. A small existing staff may, by necessity, dictate exactly the type of individual needed. A team supporting development projects often needs different skills than a team supporting production systems.

1.2.1 Positions Are Not Slots to Be Filled While it can be tempting to think of available positions as slots waiting to be filled, or to think only about tasks that will be completed once the position is filled, this is an unwise approach to hiring. The hiring process is an opportunity to build a team, taking advantage of each opportunity to hire the best individual for the needs to be satisfied. When a new staff member is hired, a complete person is added to your organization, not just a head, hands, or good ideas. Work style, career goals, personal likes, dislikes, needs, and desires are each a part of what is added to your organization. Consideration of all aspects of applicants, not just technical skills, will result in the selection of the candidate who best fits your organization.

1.2.2 People Are Dynamic People are dynamic; they change with time. Their interests and skill sets change. They become interested in new things and disinterested in old ones. They form new working relationships and sometimes new work habits. They have new responsibilities and aspire to new goals. Consideration of change in existing team members and in your organization can play a role in the hiring process.

The needs of current staff affect the hiring process. Current staff are sometimes ready, willing, and able to step into new roles, leaving slightly different areas of need in their wake. A good way to encourage this dynamic nature is to place staff in positions that give them the opportunity to have new responsibilities and grow.

1.2.3 Timing of Hiring There are cycles in the year when hiring is good, and others when it is not as good. Finding entry-level staff can best be accomplished just before college graduations, if there are no time constraints on the hiring process. American Thanksgiving, Christmas, and the New Year time frame can be a particularly good or bad time, depending on the circumstances of potential candidates. Some applicants do not want to introduce the stress of looking for a new job at holiday time. Other applicants, particularly the unemployed, are as eager to look for a new job at the holidays as they are at any other time.

Timing considerations must also include what is happening within your organization. If the interview procedure is near to holidays, it may be difficult to assemble the entire interview team. Hiring near reorganizations can introduce an additional stress in a group. Being aware of potential timing barriers in the completion of the hiring process, both from the view of the applicant and of the organization, will help arrange the timing of the hiring process as well as its timely completion. These issues can include:

- Relocation logistics for families, especially those with school age children
- Immigration and visa status arrangements
- Non-salary benefits
- Holidays
- Project deadlines and the internal company schedule
- Current economic outlook

Timely completion of the interview and hiring process is important; it is often a direct result of an expressed and urgent need. Applicants appreciate a timely follow-up to their submission of their application or resume, as well as after each following interview step. The timely selection of a candidate is a positive benefit for the group and the organization as a whole.

1.2.4 Cooperation of Current Staff When new staff are being hired, it is particularly helpful for the current staff to be excited about the introduction of new staff. The careful presentation of new positions and the description of vacancies can influence the willingness of existing staff to participate in the process. Current staff might be interested in applying for new positions if the responsibilities are in areas in which they would like to grow. If current staff are involved in the development of new position descriptions and the hiring process, they are often able to grow naturally into new duties, leaving different responsibilities available for new hires.

1.2.5 Internal vs. External Selection Organizations have varying guidelines concerning hiring from within the organization, providing opportunities for career advancement or change. It is important to understand your organization's method for handling these kinds of transfers. The Human Resources (HR) department at your organization can provide information about internal posting requirements for available positions. They might have a list of people interested in applying for jobs in the area of system administration.

It can sometimes be beneficial to accept a transfer from another part of the organization. An internal candidate will have familiarity with the organization as a whole, and still bring fresh skills to your particular group. Internal candidates have the potential for a shorter integration period because of their history with the organization. For internal candidates making career changes, you can select a candidate who doesn't have exactly the skill set originally desired, and provide appropriate training. There is a trade-off in the start-up time between a candidate with organization familiarity who needs some skill training, and a candidate possessing the skill set being sought, but unfamiliar with the organization. Understanding both the long- and short-term needs for the new position will help decide this issue.

If an internal candidate is chosen for the position, there can be an effect on the morale of internal candidates not selected. For some, having another internal candidate selected is a motivating factor for trying again in the future. For others not being selected can be a demoralizing event. There is no way to know how unselected internal candidates will react to the advancement of others, but be aware that this is a possible influence.

Don't be surprised or disappointed if internal candidates don't interview well or aren't well suited for the open position. Perhaps they lack interview skills or interpersonal skills necessary for the new position. Lack of these skills doesn't mean they are unsuited for their current positions. In fact, the experience can help them understand and value the contributions that they are making in their current jobs.

2.0 Before You Begin

The first steps in the hiring process are recognizing and justifying the need to hire. It is important both to assess and to document the need for recruitment. Evaluation should be made of a variety of issues. These include:

■ Current projects
■ Current staffing
■ Current skill sets
■ Current deficiencies
■ Desired skills

These issues should be evaluated in light of the vision for the group and future projects. If the responsibilities are focused primarily on one platform, expertise on other platforms is a bonus. If the future holds a multi-vendor environment, building expertise in a range of areas is a necessity. Help characterize the position by developing short-, medium-, and long-term views of the responsibilities of the system administration team.

2.1 Recognizing the Need to Hire

There are several conditions where the need to hire can be realized:

■ The loss of an existing staff member
■ The inability to complete projects in a timely fashion
■ The inability to complete project details
■ Stresses on existing staff
■ Stresses on existing systems
■ New project assignments
■ New service offerings

Each of these conditions can have a different impact on the type of individual finally chosen. For example, if group projects lack documentation, hiring an individual with excellent documentation skills can be appropriate. If an experienced group member leaves, younger staff might take responsibility for some of the more difficult tasks, placing the vacant position on a lower level.

The need and reasons for hiring can also impact the urgency of the hiring search. Filling a position slated to cover new service offerings is sometimes less urgent than filling a position in support of a critical organization-wide service. A short-term project may have a more urgent hiring need than a long-term project. Be aware that the amount of time needed to identify and select a candidate for a position varies with the type of position being filled.

2.1.1 Assess the State of Current Systems and Staff An overview or inventory of current projects and support commitments can provide information about necessary resources. Answers to the following questions will give some perspective on the urgency of the hiring need.

- Is documentation of the project complete?
- What is the ratio of supported machines to system administrators?
- What is the average time to answer questions or resolve problems?
- Are all machines at the current level of OS/patches/organization standard?
- How many staff members failed to take a vacation last year?
- How many staff work more than n hours per week (where n is the standard for your organization)?

Tracking these questions over time will document trends so the need for future staffing changes can be anticipated. It is beneficial to set staffing level goals for three months to a year.

An important consideration in hiring is determining the level of expertise that staff should attain in three months, six months, a year, and three years. Understanding the long-term, overall vision of projects, as well as the short-term needs, helps when articulating the need to hire. Continued growth of staff can have an impact that is different from the replacement of a single staff member. You may need to be more selective and search longer for exactly the right individual if only one opening is available and no future openings are in view. If you know that another position will soon be available, it might be appropriate to hire a good applicant who doesn't exactly fit the description. Flexibility in this area varies. Universities have needs that are different from firms that perform contract work; these can be different from large corporations with long-term support needs. Understanding your system administration needs and having a vision for future projects are key to hiring the right individual.

2.2 Authorization to Recruit

Each organization has a different process and procedure for authorizing a recruitment. This can vary from deciding if there is enough work and sufficient funds to hire, to a complicated set of procedures and paperwork to be completed. Know the regulations that your organization has in place for the hiring process. The Human Relations office may take many steps on your behalf. Be aware of any governmental regulations in effect for your local area or industry. By taking full advantage of existing processes, both time and effort can be saved.

2.3 Company Policies and Procedures

Company policies and procedures can be both a help and a hindrance to the hiring process. Accepting that they exist and using them to benefit the process can make them less of a hindrance. Know who is responsible for each part of the hiring process to eliminate unnecessary duplication of effort and to prevent situations that arise when individuals do too much or not enough in the hiring process.

Check with the HR department at your organization about current or new procedures before beginning recruitment. You need to learn the current regulations, as well as find out about recent revisions, before beginning the process. For example:

- Do you have current copies of all necessary forms?
- Do all applicants need to fill out a standard application, or are a cover letter and resume sufficient?
- Are there any forms that need to be processed after the search is complete?
- Are there time constraints on any of the steps in the process?

It may be necessary for you to handle the interface with the HR department directly, or administrative help may be available in your department, or the HR department might handle many of the hiring details on your behalf. Abiding by procedures, knowing the deadlines, and having all hiring materials complete will make the process the most efficient – though never painless.

2.4 Assess the Corporate Culture

It is important to understand the culture of your organization before beginning the hiring process. You will need to look at both the local group or team in which the individual will work and the larger overall organization. Understanding your own environment will help you select employees who will fit well in your workplace. Because there are a variety of work settings, consider what best describes your workplace:

- Conservative, Moderate, or Liberal
- Confrontational or Cooperative
- Driven or Relaxed
- Polished, Down-to-earth, or Dilbert

- Interrupt Driven or Proactive
- Left Brain or Right Brain

Understand your own management style:

- Do you need or have much interaction with your staff?
- Do you need or have significant day-to-day control over projects?
- What kind of supervision does your existing staff want and get?
- What kind of support do you get from your own supervisor?

Once you understand the culture of your workplace, you can decide whether to choose an applicant who will be more of the same or to test the edge and choose an individual who is somewhat different. Selecting an individual with the necessary technical skills will not guarantee the individual's happiness in the new organization nor your organization's satisfaction with the newcomer. Technical skills alone are not enough to make the organization happy with the new staff member. The overall organizational fit must be considered if the hiring process is going to have a successful result.

2.5 Opportunities for Change

Hiring new staff can be an excellent opportunity to introduce a little bit of change to your organization. The size of your current staff will determine how much difference is noticed with the introduction of a new employee. Sometimes an organization cannot afford to introduce too much diversity or accept anything less than a perfect match, because this can unnecessarily upset the environment. Introduce change by considering particular areas of expertise, work style, and the backgrounds of both the candidate and the current group.

For example, introducing a programmer with large project experience into a group of system administrators can provide new skills for project management and documentation that might previously have been weak or lacking. Hiring an individual with pre-sales support experience can introduce both polish and public relations skills into a group that previously lacked these qualities. The introduction of change does not have to be dramatic; small variations in skill sets can produce big growth for existing staff members.

2.6 Position Description

Development of the position description before recruiting is a helpful tool in the identification of the individual who is to be hired. The HR department at your organization may have a process for creating position descriptions, or might prepare them on your behalf. Check with them to be sure of the division of these responsibilities.

The position description serves two functions. It is a tool for the employer to use when identifying a potential employee and it is a tool for candidates to use when making their decision about accepting future employment. A clear and complete position description can translate into an advertisement that will attract appropriate applicants. Developing a complete description of the duties, technical background, and expectations improves the chances of finding the right individual.

Make a list of required and preferred skills in advance and if possible, circulate this list among current employees and peers for comment before the hiring process begins. Their input will be an important resource in the definition of the position. It will reveal their points of view on the group's strengths and weaknesses, and it will help current employees understand what is being sought in new employees. Developing a complete description of the duties, technical background, and expectations, and having it reviewed improves the chances of finding the best individual.

2.6.1 Technical Areas of Expertise When developing both the position description and the advertisement, it is important to have a clear understanding of the technical skills being sought. While it isn't always possible to find a perfect match, it is important to have a minimum baseline and an acceptable skill set.

The exact list of skills needed varies from position to position and organization to organization. For system administrators, the skill sets can include adding users, building kernels, software installation, and database administration. The level and complexity of each position dictates the technical skills detailed in the position description. To clarify the evaluation of the candidates, indicate whether a skill is required or preferred.

It is tempting to focus only on the areas of technical expertise needed in the new employee. While technical expertise is important, it is not the only area to be considered. When developing the position descriptions, it can be sufficient to survey the current projects and list the skills needed. Be specific when writing your technical requirements:

- If Solaris support is needed, then say that.
- If general skills are the focus, and the focus is on platform independence, say so.
- If some skills are required and others only preferred, make sure that they are appropriately categorized.
- If all the programming and scripting is done in PERL, make sure the candidate knows PERL, rather than general scripting languages.

The balance between what is really needed, and what is preferred is important because if a required skill isn't appropriately emphasized, an inappropriate candidate could be selected. Try not to overload the description so that no applicant can fit the bill and in turn, no one applies. If too few skills are listed, the selected candidate might be unable to perform the required work.

The SAGE booklet *Job Descriptions for System Administrators* (2nd edition, 1997) gives a general framework for describing various levels of skills. Some position postings say simply SAGE Level 2, and assume that applicants will know what this means. It is helpful to describe the most important skills necessary for a position at that level. This saves applicants who are not familiar with the various levels from having to figure out if they are qualified. It also saves the reviewer of the applications from having to reject applications that were sent in error. Qualified applicants might not apply at all if they can't understand the posting. As a general goal, make the position description and subsequent advertisements as clear, complete, and inviting as possible.

2.6.2 Interpersonal Expertise There are many non-technical skills to consider when developing the position description. Interpersonal skills are important for any position. However, focus on the skills that are most necessary for the position. Consider the following list:

- Communication skills: If the individual will be working closely with others, communication skills are necessary. These can range from meeting skills to conflict resolution.
- Public speaking: If the individual will be giving presentations of any type, say so.
- Negotiation: If the position requires negotiation with vendors, or clients, make sure to list these skills.
- Leadership: The level of leadership will depend on the level of the job. Junior level positions do not always require leadership skills.
- Time management: This is related to work style. How much flexibility will an employee have in determining pace of work? How much supervision will there be?

If the group is in desperate need of excellent technical skills, it may be necessary to favor technical skills over interpersonal skills. The weight assigned to each set of skills varies from position to position and opportunity to opportunity. Be aware that these can be both competing and complementary areas. Appendix C includes some sample questions.

2.6.3 Work Style and Independence The predominant work style in the group can be an important factor in selecting the best candidate. The position description should include some information about preferred work style and level of independence along with any other necessary work style details. Consider the following issues:

- How much day to day supervision does this position receive? This can be stated as a percentage.
- Should the candidates have experience with trouble ticket systems?
- Will the candidates have access to sensitive data?
- What are the consequences of unintentional disclosure of data?
- Will security clearance be necessary?

Carefully review your environment to be certain that the most important areas are included in the position description.

2.6.4 The Evaluation Tool After making, circulating, and reviewing the lists of technical, interpersonal, and work style skills that the ideal candidate should possess, it is time to develop an evaluation tool. Comparing candidates side by side on various skills will give an idea about how candidates measure up against the ideal candidate and with each other. Appendix B contains a sample evaluation tool.

Part of this tool can be used to have each candidate complete a self-evaluation on a variety of skills. This self-evaluation can be part of an application form filled out by each candidate before the interview takes place. Knowing how applicants view their own strong and weak skills can be a guide during the interview process.

A self-evaluation tool can be used in the interview process, or it can be used in the review process where the interview team sees the self-evaluation only after seeing the candidate. If the self-evaluation is to be available during the interview process, each applicant will need to fill it out before the interview so that the interview team can have time to review it before seeing the applicant. If it is only to be used during the review process, have the applicant fill it out as a first stop at the first personal interview. Alternatively, the self-evaluation can be given in a verbal form. For example:

- On a scale of one to five (one low, five high) how would you rank yourself on . . .
- Do you prefer to work with . . .
  no supervision, some supervision, frequent supervision?
- What is the most difficult [some situation] for you?
  Why is it difficult?

If applicants complete self-evaluations in any form, be sure you understand the purpose of collecting the information.

- Will it be used as a double check for answers to interview questions?
- Will it be used to evaluate the range of knowledge?
- Is it used to complete an overall view of the candidate?

Appendix B contains a sample evaluation tool.

2.7 When to Look

Once the preliminary work is completed, evaluate the timing of the hiring. In some organizations, the timing of hiring is dependent on current deadline schedules, vacation and training schedules of staff, and availability of individuals to participate on the search and selection committee. If the HR department is directly involved, their availability and schedules can also impact the recruitment time line. Candidates may wish to see an operation in full production. For example, the flavor of a university campus is different when classes are in session. As mentioned earlier, searching for candidates near holiday times can be difficult. Sometimes there is no flexibility in the timing of the recruitment process. If a staff member leaves and work becomes stalled waiting on resources, hiring must proceed as quickly as possible. Remember that organizational work done in advance saves time in the process and grief afterwards when the best candidate is selected on the first try. Hiring can also be viewed as an on-going process. Keep recruitment materials up to date and position description templates available to speed up future hiring processes.

2.8 Search Committee

Although using a search committee may appear to lengthen the interview process, many benefits are obtained by including a selected range of expertise on the committee.

There are a variety of interview styles, including group, individual personal interviews, and a combination of these. Select the interview style that fits both you and your organization. Discuss interview styles with committee members and management to be sure that everyone is comfortable with the process. Check with the HR department in your organization to see if there are procedures in place to help facilitate the interview process.

There are advantages and disadvantages to different sized committees. Scheduling, varying points of view, and the need to include co-workers and clients are all important considerations. People who say "me too" or "whatever you want" may appear to be the path of least resistance, but they won't necessarily help in the selection of the best candidate. Similarly, argumentative individuals can be an unnecessary barrier in the search process. Choose committee members who speak up and provide constructive input.

2.8.1 Interview and Selection Committees Some organizations use an interview committee to evaluate the skills of each applicant and a smaller selection committee for final candidate selection. In other organizations, the interview committee makes a recommendation to the hiring manager, or the director of a division. Some organizations use the same set of people for the interview committee and the selection committee. It is important to be aware of how your organization handles the interview process, and to work within the system to select the best possible candidate.

2.8.2 Developing the Committee In forming the committee, include individuals who are able to evaluate each of the necessary skill areas. If the position requires someone with Solaris, AIX, and PERL experience, at least one committee member must be able to evaluate these areas. If no one is available on your staff or organization with these skills, be willing to draw on resources from outside your area. If the candidate must possess a mix of technical skills and customer service skills, consider asking one of your customers to participate on the interview committee. You may want to consider including, or you may be required to include, your own supervisor. If your supervisor does not directly participate in the interview process, take the time to get your supervisor's input on the position description. Check with your supervisor for insight into your skills and the strengths and weaknesses of your group of which you might not be aware.

Consider including a representative from the following areas:

- A peer
- A client
- Your supervisor
- A technical evaluator
- An interpersonal evaluator
- Yourself

The individuals included on the search committee will depend upon availability and interest. When asking people to participate on the committee, be sure to ask them how much time they are able to spend. A committee member who can spend only 10-15 minutes with each candidate is unlikely to provide much valuable input. Offer to be available to others when they need a committee. Building a network of people with whom you can share recruiting responsibilities is a practical way to build a effective hiring process.

2.8.3 Committee Communication The committee should meet together at least once before seeing any candidates. This allows committee members to understand the goals of the process and their roles in the process, and to meet other members whom they don't know. It allows a time for discussion before the candidates are posed any questions.

It is handy to have a single record (paper or electronic) which includes the names, addresses, phone numbers, and email addresses of each of the committee members. All committee members should be given a complete copy of each candidate's interview schedule. This is important even if the interviews are being conducted in a group panel style.

Some committees discuss candidates after the completion of each interview; others wait until all candidates have been interviewed. It is recommended that the follow-up discussion of each candidate takes place soon after the interview, so that details remain fresh in the minds of the committee members and confusion about candidates does not occur. Hold a final committee meeting to complete the final ranking of the candidates, and to discuss reasons for accepting or rejecting candidates.

2.8.4 Interview Styles There can be several levels of interviews, including phone screening of applicants, testing, first interviews, luncheon interviews, and final interviews. Some organizations administer a test to applicants to check their skills, while others explicitly forbid this practice. Check with the HR department to find out what practices are commonly followed, or if there are any practices expressly required or forbidden in your organization.

Have a set of questions prepared in advance of any interview, and pose the same or a similar set of questions to each candidate. This gives a baseline from which to evaluate the candidates. Know what you hope to learn from each question asked. A question that doesn't provide useful information about a candidate is a question not worth asking.

If individual interviews are used, it is often beneficial to have questions repeated by more than one of the committee members. This allows for checking the consistency of a candidate's answers. If a group interview is conducted, it is important to understand that the candidates will likely be nervous. Have the committee prearrange the list of questions and the assignment of questions to help the interview flow smoothly. The more relaxed the committee members are, the more relaxed the candidates will be. In the group interview style, a round table setting can be more relaxing for the candidate than a panel setting.

Sometimes it is appropriate and helpful to conclude a morning interview with an informal lunch. This can provide additional time for discussion of specific areas and it is a less formal way to become more acquainted with the candidates. As candidates relax, more natural conversations can occur and you can obtain a better overall view.

2.8.5 *Interview Skills* Being the interviewer isn't necessarily any easier than being the candidate. The guidelines for being a good interviewer are much the same as they are for being a good candidate:

- Be on time.
- Know the name of the candidate.
- State your name clearly.
- Be polite.
- Be prepared.
- Be neat.
- Make eye contact.
- Don't talk too much.

It is important to phrase questions so that the question does not contain an answer that can be repeated by a candidate. It is also important to phrase questions so that they cannot be answered with a simple yes or no. Consider the differences among the following questions:

- Did you ever have problems installing sendmail?
- Did you find that sendmail.cf files were difficult to configure when installing sendmail?
- Tell me about a difficult problem you encountered installing sendmail.

Asking brief questions with yes/no answers, and following up with more probing questions, allows candidates to elaborate on an experience or why they like or dislike something. Questions that begin "Tell me about" give the candidate an opportunity to discuss issues. When personal experiences are being related, there is less chance for the candidates to feel that they aren't giving the right answer.

Many candidates will be well prepared for the interview process and some may even try to have the interviewer do most of the talking. Remember that the evaluation is a two-way process; you are evaluating the candidates and they are evaluating your organization. It is appropriate for candidates to have questions, but don't spend so much time answering a candidate's questions that there is no time is left for you to ask questions. If a candidate cannot follow a discussion topic, dominates the conversation, or talks about things not necessarily related to the question at hand, that candidate might be difficult to supervise. A candidate's ability to follow your lead in the interview process can be an indicator of ability and willingness to accept guidance as an employee.

2.8.6 Lack of Interview Skills Both the candidate and interviewer need to possess interviewing skills. If you haven't interviewed candidates before, and feel that you don't have the skills necessary for conducting an effective interview, read books on interviewing skills, and develop questions to ask candidates. You will want to practice before interviewing for the first time. Ask a co-worker or friend to role play a practice interview with you, much as you would if you were a candidate for a job, but reversing the roles.

Ask if you can sit in and observe a more experienced interviewer, perhaps in another department or for a recruitment in which you are not on the hiring team. Don't participate in the interview, but be observant of the actions of the interviewer and the reactions of the candidate. Make sure you have a pad and pen so that you can take notes about how the interviewer relates to the candidate and about the phrasing of the questions. These observations will help you in developing your own interview technique. If you have the opportunity to observe a group interview, you may be asked to sit on the side (rather than at the table), so you will need to be observant about how each participant interacts with the candidate.

If interviewing is going to be a large part of your duties, consider getting formal training, to make you more comfortable with your role in the process. If formal training isn't an option, consider less costly options such as reading books or role playing. Practicing doesn't have to cost money, it just takes time.

2.8.7 Lack of Technical Knowledge It isn't necessary to be a technical manager to be a successful manager of system administrators. It is necessary to understand the issues that system administrators face in their day-to-day work. If you don't possess skills necessary to evaluate the technical background of candidates, you will need to find a reliable source of help for this task. There are several avenues to be explored, including:

- Using one of your existing staff as a search committee member
- Drawing on resources from elsewhere in your organization
- Using an employment agency to do the initial technical screening

Whatever methods you choose, you will need to be satisfied that the technical skills of the candidates were fully evaluated and are at the level that the position demands.

3.0 **Publicizing the Position**

Once the position description is completed, and the committee members identified, it is time to begin the search for the best possible candidates. Sometimes it's sufficient to look within the larger organization for a candidate who is already on the payroll and functioning in a different capacity. Sometimes it is appropriate to look within the local community to find an individual with the skills needed. This can be within the geographic community or the corporate community. For example, a candidate for a system administration position at a large corporation could potentially come from a smaller company. Using both traditional advertising venues and informal networking is particularly important when a national or international search is performed.

3.1 Informal Networking

Using the informal network in a vigorous way can sometimes produce the best candidates. Individuals whom you have met at conferences could have suggestions about potential candidates or could be appropriate candidates. Consider sending a prepared position description to some close colleagues. Ask them to refer anyone whom they think is appropriate. Use the HR department to contact employment agencies and placement offices at appropriate colleges and universities.

The size of your organization will play a role in the variety of options that can be used in identifying candidates. Participating in local job fairs by sending representatives to talk about your organization can be a way to identify potential candidates on an ongoing basis. If the hiring need is large, it may be possible to hold an open house at your organization. If your organization has an annual open house, use that as an opportunity to highlight your department and the desire to hire. The use of non-traditional resources, including electronic forums, is particularly appropriate for locating system administrators, since they often circulate in the electronic environment. Having electronic copies of the job posting freely available will assist in this area. However, if the competition for system administrators in your area is high, these less aggressive methods could be ineffective.

3.2 The Advertisement

Placement, wording, and the number of advertisements placed is directly related to the amount of money available for the hiring process. In some organizations this is not an issue; in others, money is a large concern. It is common to spend 10%-20% of the annual salary of a system administration position in recruiting expenses, including advertising and travel expenses of candidates. In addition, reviewing resumes, setting up interviews, interviewing and discussion of candidates can take a significant portion of staff time.

The goal of an advertisement is to attract the ideal candidate. As in developing the position description, enough information should be included so that potential candidates know what kind of individual (or skill set) is being sought and what compensation is offered. Lack of information in an advertisement can cause qualified candidates to skip over the position. Qualified candidates might not apply if they need to call or write for more information about the position. Too many requirements can discourage good candidates from applying if they don't have all the skills listed, even though the position requires only a subset of the skills. A successful advertisement is clear, complete, and inviting.

3.2.1 Where and When to Place an Advertisement Placement of an advertisement is a fundamental factor in reaching the candidates. If no one knows a position is available in your organization, no one can apply. There are a variety of methods available, including:

- Existing internal organizational mechanisms (HR)
  The HR division at your organization may have a variety of resources that can be used for placing an advertisement.
- Traditional print media – newspapers and magazines
  Some newspapers are affiliated with electronic searches such as *careerpath.com*, while others have Web-based versions of their help wanted section. Be sure to ask if an electronic version of the print advertisement can be placed at the same time as the print version, and if there is any additional cost for this service. Some newspapers and magazines have particular days, weeks or special issues that are dedicated to technology-related jobs. It is worth asking if these specialty sections are a part of the paper or magazine in which advertising space is purchased.
- Electronic mailing lists
  There are many electronic mailing lists and news groups that focus solely on job postings. Understand the etiquette of each list or newsgroup you plan to use before you prepare and send the advertisement. Some lists require that a particular format be used or that specific information be included with each posting, or have a limit on the number of postings, or limit the type that can be sent at any time. Remember that sage-jobs-offered and the USENIX SAGE Web page are excellent resources for advertising for system administrators.

■ World Wide Web postings
Consider your organization's own Web site for posting job positions with links to specific groups or projects so that candidates can obtain information about your organization.

Consider registering your organization with an electronic job search agency such as *monsterboard.com* or *occ.com*, or find out about the Department of Labor Web site in your state. System administrators are likely to search electronically for a new position. Making the open position in your organization visible opens new possibilities for attracting candidates.

■ Job search agencies
If system administration is new in your organization, using a job search agency to identify and attract appropriate candidates can be an effective strategy.

Each of these methods reaches a different section of the community and varies in cost. No matter what combination of methods is chosen for the advertisement, it is best to use the same (or similar) description in each mechanism. You can obtain information about the success of each advertisement, even if the candidates neglect to mention where they saw the position posting, by using a slightly different reply address in each advertisement. This information will help you focus your efforts in future recruitments. Take advantage of as many resources as possible without overloading the recruitment process to produce the most attractive set of applicants and in turn, perhaps, the best-fit employees.

3.2.2 Keywords One key to getting appropriate candidates to apply for the position is to include keywords to act as attractors rather than detractors in the position. Asking for specific skills generally produces applicants with skills that are appropriate for the position. Asking for "System Administration skills" doesn't help the candidates know whether someone with UNIX or NT skills is needed, or if there is some preferred flavor of UNIX. If the position requires a PERL expert, make sure to mention this, rather than writing "scripting language expertise." Carefully check the wording of the advertisement before posting it. You don't want to ask for 10-15 years of PERL or Java experience by mistake.

4.0 Initial Review of Applicants' Materials

Have a plan in place for evaluating the applications, before advertisements are placed and applications begin to arrive. Applications or resumes can be reviewed as they arrive. They can be reviewed in groups, perhaps weekly, or if your organization has a formal posting period, they can all be reviewed at the end of the period. Choose a method that works best for the timing of the recruitment and for the normal processing in your organization. The initial review of applicants is best accomplished by a small group of people to save both time and effort. Use an evaluation tool to eliminate applicants who do not meet the minimum requirements, and separate the superior candidates from those who are minimally qualified. Appendix B contains a sample evaluation tool.

4.1 Minimum Requirements

Minimum requirements vary among both positions and organizations. The SAGE booklet *Job Descriptions for System Administrators* (2nd edition, 1997) includes good baseline descriptions from which applications can evaluated. These combined with the position description serve as guidelines for the first-pass evaluation. Items to consider as minimum requirements include:

- Formal degrees
- Other formal training
- Informal training
- Years of experience
- Types of experience
- Previous responsibilities
- Specific skills

It is important to distinguish between amount of experience and the type of experience. An applicant may have many years of computer experience but no experience appropriate for the system administration position in your organization.

5.0 The Interview Process

Once an initial evaluation of the candidate applications is complete, the interview process can begin. Be sure to check with the HR department to find out if any local or corporate requirements exist for the interview process. There may be a policy and process in place in your organization that completely determines how interviews are to be handled. If flexibility is permissible, decide which interview style works best for you and your committee. Determine your time frame for the various stages of the interview process, and be aware of any potential barriers that may exist in the completion of this phase.

The display of power and the unnerving of candidates are not appropriate at an interview. It is best to help candidates be at ease, rather than on edge. As an interviewer, you are presenting your organization to potential employees, and these potential employees are learning about your organization. Because of the nature of the field of system administration, it is interesting and perhaps beneficial to know how a candidate will react in an unknown or difficult situation, but it is not necessary to make the interview process any more difficult than necessary.

5.1 Legal and Illegal Questions

The HR department should be able to supply you with any requirements or guidelines for your company. It can be challenging to phrase questions to learn specific information, without violating the rights of the candidates. For example, you shouldn't ask a applicant's native language; however, asking applicants about their ability to read, speak or write languages that are job-related is relevant.

5.2 Tests

If the candidates will be required to take a test or give a presentation, inform them of this ahead of time. Testing candidates can be a complicated issue. Testing ranges from written examinations, to verbal exchanges, to demonstrations of skills. In some states, a written test is not permitted, unless it was certified that the test instrument is not biased towards or against any group of individuals. The simplest method is often to use verbal queries, in the guise of conversation.

If a test of any sort is going to be administered, make sure you know ahead of time what will be learned from the results. For example, does the test reveal:

- The limits of problem solving skills
- The candidate's depth of skills
- The candidate's breadth of skills
- Particular knowledge
- General knowledge

You don't want to come away from the exercise with a gut feeling, no demonstrable results and no empirical way to rank the candidates. Make sure that the results can be objectively judged, so that a concrete mechanism can be used for ranking the applicants.

5.3 Telephone Interviews

Conducting telephone interviews separates marginal candidates from acceptable ones without placing a major burden on the applicants, yourself, or the interview team. In a telephone interview, cover material that is not clearly available from the application or resume. The questions should be covered in about 20-30 minutes. Prepare the questions ahead of time, and write them out for easy reference. Take notes during the interview, and write the answers directly onto your question sheet. Having a clear goal of what is being evaluated or learned about each applicant during the telephone part of the interview will help with the next step, the personal interviews. Appendix C provides some possible questions.

5.4 Personal Interviews

Once you have selected candidates for personal interviews, determine with your committee how the interviews will take place, and set up the interview schedule. The urgency of the need to hire will drive the timing of the interviews. If the position needs to be filled immediately, you will want to limit the interviewing to the best candidates and see them as quickly as possible. If time is less of an issue, you can expand the search and see more candidates. It is important to see all candidates in a timely fashion. Good system administrators find jobs quickly.

If administrative staff is available to arrange the interviews, use that resource. Since the interview process can be exhausting for interviewers as well as candidates, time should be set aside for the hiring process. Try not to have interviews wedged between other meetings or into a generally busy schedule. It is better to set aside blocks of time in the scheduling of the interviews to allow flexibility, and reduce the general stress of the process on the interview team.

5.4.1 Aim for a Positive Experience When the personal interview is scheduled, the candidates should be given an overview of the interview process. Provide candidates with a map and complete directions on how to find the interview site. One hotly debated topic is proper interview attire. Provide the candidates with information about whether your organization has a casual or formal environment and appropriate dress for the interview. Some may decide to decline further interviews based on dress requirements.

Early clarification of such an issue can save time for both your interview team and the applicants. Providing this information lets candidates know that you are interested in seeing them succeed. These simple, preliminary details help set the tone for the upcoming personal interview, and puts your organization in its best light.

The personal interview is a chance for candidates to make their best impression on you and your organization, and for you to make the best effort to sell the available position to candidates. It is a time of mutual buying and selling. You will want to make the candidates feel comfortable, and that their time was well spent at the interview. You want your organization to look as attractive as possible, because while you currently may be hiring only one individual, you may want to draw from the same pool of candidates in the future. Candidates who have good interview experiences might recommend your organization to others based on their positive interview experiences.

5.4.2 The Interview Setting The setting for the interview should be quiet and comfortable. If a group interview is used, a conference room of suitable size with the resources needed should be reserved well in advance. Check the status of the room before the interview to avert any last-minute problems. If individual interviews are used, make sure that each interviewer has a location free from interruptions, including telephones and pagers.

5.4.3 First Personal Interview While the telephone interview helps identify candidates who are minimally qualified, the first personal interview will clarify the ranking of the candidates. It is also the applicant's opportunity to get to know you and your organization. It is important to be well organized for this part of the process. Have your question set prepared ahead of time, preferably on a clipboard that can be held in your lap for note taking. This keeps your notations out of the eye range of the applicant and will be less distracting. Appendix C contains sample questions.

Eye contact and body language give important clues about how each applicant copes with the interview process. These aren't the most important factors, but they can give telling clues. An overconfident physical appearance can be an overcompensation for insecurities. Failure to make and hold eye contact can be an indicator of an inability to meet challenges; in system administration, challenges are frequent.

The candidate should be introduced to each member of the interview team and be told how each team member fits in the organization. This can be done in several ways. If the interview is done in a group, team members can introduce themselves and briefly state their position in the organization. If individual interviews are held, the first individual greeting the candidate can give an interview schedule to the candidate with each team member's name and job title, as well as the time for each interview. For example, a 3x5 card with information such as:

Mary Smith	Hiring Manager	10:00A.M.-10:30A.M.
Dave Jackson	UNIX System Administrator	10:45A.M.-11:15A.M.
John Jones	Network Manager	11:30A.M.-12 noon
Mary Smith	Hiring Manager	12:15P.M.-12:45P.M.

Note the 15 minute slack time between interviews; this is so that candidates have a chance to go to the rest room or pull their wits together, and to cover travel time between offices.

The personal interview is used to reconfirm technical skills and to evaluate fit within the organization. Helping candidates feel comfortable not only provides them an opportunity to present their best, but gives the interviewer an opportunity to learn more about skills and personalities.

5.4.4 Final Personal Interview Final interviews are most commonly reserved for candidates of the highest quality or candidates who will have project leadership or management responsibility. This step in the interview process may include other members of management and additional clients or co-workers. It is generally used as a last check, to make sure everyone is comfortable with the selected candidates and that no last minute surprises arise.

Provide interviewers with information from previous steps in the interview process so that previously covered material won't be covered again by accident. However, repeating questions deliberately allows for a double check of candidates' answers.

A disadvantage of a multi-step interview process is that candidates will need to visit your company site repeatedly. This is often difficult for candidates currently employed or for candidates from out of town. Since it is likely that candidates will only be brought in from a distance when they are genuine contenders for the position, it is best to schedule all interviews for a single visit. But such visits may be spread over more than one day.

6.0 Evaluating the Candidates

The bulk of the interview process involves the evaluation and ranking of each candidate. Having a method in place for evaluating candidates before starting the review process will allow for an objective review of required and desired skills. Again, knowing ahead of time the type of position that needs to be filled and the kind of candidate who needs to be attracted will help in determining when the right individual has been identified.

For each area considered, there isn't necessarily a right or wrong answer, but rather an acceptable range. Technically correct answers should also have the elegance of the solution evaluated. This is why it is important to understand the characteristics being sought and the limits of acceptability. When considering answers to technical questions consider:

- Did the solution use multiple tools?
- Where did these tools originate?
- Was it a brute force method?
- Was there a simpler way?
- What are the breadth and depth of the personal tool set?
- What made it a good technical solution at the time?
- If the applicant didn't know the answer, was this admitted?

6.1 Second Use of the Evaluation Tool

The evaluation tool was first used to identify the candidates who met the minimum requirements. Now it helps identify those candidates who, while they appear to meet the minimum requirements, lack a fundamental skill required for filling the position. Later in the interview process, the evaluation tool will help you rank the candidates and compare various strengths and weakness. It may not be appropriate to use the same evaluation tool for every search, but do use the same tool throughout a single search. You may want to have several templates available, perhaps based on the various job description levels in the SAGE booklet *Job Descriptions for System Administrators* (2nd edition, 1997). Have a template that includes evaluation criteria for all position types in your area. Keeping these up to date for all the positions in your group will cut down on the work that needs to be done before future recruiting starts. A sample evaluation tool can be found in Appendix B.

6.2 Evaluation of Technical Expertise

Technical expertise can range from being the most important set of skills evaluated to one of the least important. Have an idea about how much and what kind of technical expertise is desired, and what is minimally needed before beginning to interview the candidates. What is needed and what is wanted are sometimes not the same. Decide ahead of time what tradeoffs can be made to secure the right candidate for the position.

Technical expertise can be demonstrated by asking candidates to:

- Solve a particular problem.
- Demonstrate skills with a hands-on situation.
- Give a short presentation on a topic.
- Discuss technical areas that are of particular relevance to the open position.

Remember that if a written test is to be given, the test must be a valid instrument, and you should know what is being demonstrated by the test results. If a less formal, discussion-type interview is held, prepare questions ahead of time, and have them available so you can take notes during the discussion for future reference. Use the evaluation tool that was developed explicitly for the position to develop questions that can be discussed with candidates and lead to additional information about both the types and depth of their skills.

Some candidates may be an acceptable match with interpersonal and work style skills but not with technical skills. For example, a candidate with AIX experience but no Solaris experience might want to know if training is available to learn Solaris administration. Some organizations have a provision for this, while others do not. Unfortunately, in small organizations, it is often not practical to hire someone who needs technical training because work must get done without too much investment. Balancing position needs with the candidate's skills will help in making this decision.

6.3 Interpersonal Skills

System administrators need to be able to interact with other system administrators, with programmers, with vendors, and with all sorts of end users. Good communication and interpersonal skills are important considerations in selecting the top candidate. Communications range from updates on system status, through documentation of installation processes and explanation of problem resolution, to user education. Evaluating interpersonal skills can be a difficult task. Questions that ask the candidate to describe situations where there was conflict, a disagreement with a co-worker or supervisor, can give insight into this area.

6.4 Problem Solving Skills

One of the bedrocks of system administration is problem solving. The ability to think clearly in difficult situations and to arrive at sensible solutions is one of the most important skills of a system administrator. Evaluation of this skill can be difficult, because unless a test or demonstration is administered, there isn't an objective way of determining what kinds of problems an individual can solve. It is possible to find out how candidates approach problems, or how they have solved problems in the past.

Ask the candidates to "tell about a time" or "describe a situation" in which they had to use their problem solving skills. This provides information on what they think is a difficult problem. It also gives information about their ability to solve the problem they described. Finally, it directly demonstrates a candidate's ability to describe problems and their solutions. When engaged in a conversation about difficult problems, be careful not to try and guess the solution that a candidate used, or be surprised when the solution is given. These questions don't have right or wrong answers, because they reflect a candidate's experiences.

6.5 Integration of Staff

Characterize the work style of the group where the new staff member will work and note each candidate's match with these characteristics to help evaluate the complementary or supplementary nature of the work styles. Integrating an individual who comes from a culture of formal written documentation into a more casual environment can pose problems for both existing and new employees. Discovering a candidate's work style preferences and background can help assess whether a smooth transition into your organization is possible. Each organization has a particular pecking order, which can be based on seniority, skill set, strength of personality or a variety of other factors. Integrating new staff smoothly into an established setting can depend on the match or mismatch of personalities and work styles.

6.6 Fit with Your Clients

System administrators interact with clients, the users of the machines they administer. Clients can range from researchers who think of their workstations the way chemists think of test tubes and beakers, to software application developers, who care about system calls and system interfaces. Application programs can also be a primary focus of a client. A system administrator with a background in fine arts or literature may or may not be appropriate for a position supporting research machines in the hard sciences. Hiring an individual with a business background could be ideal for supporting systems running business or financial applications. It is important to consider both the client users and applications when selecting a system administrator. Understanding the needs of both the users and the applications of a system will help in selecting the system administrator who is appropriate for the system.

6.7 Past Career Path

It is not uncommon for system administrators to change jobs, companies, states, and even countries frequently. The path these changes take can give an indication of how a candidate potentially fits into your organization. A candidate with a history of working on development projects might not be satisfied in a daily support position. A candidate who finds his/her current position too demanding and seeks something less rigorous could be inappropriate for a new organizational filesystem selection and implementation project. Try to understand why candidates left each job, and what benefit they were seeking in each new one.

6.8 Growth Potential and Desire

Some candidates are looking for a new career path with opportunities to learn new material, gain new skills, and perhaps move into project leadership or management responsibilities. Other candidates have little interest in leading or managing projects. Some candidates come from rock-solid support positions and are looking for more of the same, in a new environment. Matching a candidate to a career path requires understanding both growth potential and the candidate's desire for advancement.

6.8.1 Desire for Guidance In a new environment, all system administrators need an overview of policies, procedures, and methods. The level of guidance an employee receives often relates directly to the level of that employee's system administration skills. Less experienced system administrators sometimes need more guidance than those who are more experienced.

A candidate's comfort level in accepting guidance is important in the selection process. If a position requires an individual who can follow directions exactly and work in a group or with close supervision, it is inappropriate to hire someone who prefers to work in a solitary environment. Conversely, if the position requires an individual with creativity who can work alone, hiring someone who prefers to have work checked frequently would not be ideal.

6.9 Future Career Plans

You may be looking for a system administrator today, but also want that individual to grow into a future leadership role. A system administrator might be interested in joining an organization where the potential for future growth is perceived. Asking candidates what they imagine they would like to be doing in one, three and five years is a good way to gain information about the desire for growth and leadership. While system administration and technical computing fields change rapidly, most candidates can describe in an abstract fashion what they would like to be doing in the future. Creating an environment where your staff can obtain career objectives gives your organization a reputation as a place where people want to work.

6.9.1 Desire to Move into Management Understanding candidates' medium- to long-range career goals can help in determining the potential fit of each candidate into your organization. The career path available to staff influences the selection of a candidate, and a candidate's acceptance of an offer. If a candidate wants to grow into management and there is no opportunity for such a career path in your organization, then it is neither to the advantage of your organization nor to the applicant for an offer to be made. If a system administrator is being hired with the plan of development into a technical management position, make it clear to applicants that this is the future direction of this position. Some applicants have no interest in management. It is possible to avoid having a mismatch from the start by discussing future plans.

6.10 Work Style

Work style preferences can impact how a candidate fits into your organization. Some individuals are innovative in their problem solving technique, others are adaptive. Some prefer a fixed work schedule, others prefer flexibility. Some work in a neat and orderly workspace, others work in what appears to be chaos. Some handle many assignments at one time with ease, others prefer to handle fewer projects at one time. The hours of your production environment, the product produced, and your organization's culture all contribute to the personality of your organization. Some candidates may be willing and able to adjust their work style to your workplace and some may not.

One aspect of system administration related to work style is long-term versus short-term projects. Long-term projects include the maintenance of systems, including upgrades, day-to-day maintenance, user support, and the development and installation of new systems. For example, the research and design of a new system for handling mail delivery has a different flavor and length than the maintenance of a production mail delivery system. Many system administrators have a clear preference for the length of time that they like to spend on particular types of tasks. Some prefer to change projects frequently, others like to settle in for the long term. During the interview, be sure to discuss work style preferences and adaptations as well as the types of projects available.

6.11 Support Systems

The support system available to a candidate is often not directly visible on a resume, but it should be checked during the interview process. Much of system administration is related to problem solving, and some problems need more than one head to solve. Having knowledge of and ability to tap other resources for problem solving can increase a candidate's performance potential.

For example, if a position being filled has a security slant:

- Do the candidates subscribe to various security mailing lists?
- Are they aware of them? Are they participants?
- Do they find some particular news groups beneficial? Which ones?
- Have they attended any security workshops or conferences?

System administrators working at sites that don't have news feeds might not know which news groups have useful information, but access to mailing lists is available at most sites.

A network of friends and former coworkers, as well as participation in local professional organizations, can indicate the resources available to a candidate. Personal literature collections, including books and magazines, can give some information about how an applicant learns new material and attacks problems. Ask candidates about the most recent technical book or magazine they read and what they learned from it. Ask how it helped in solving a current problem or project.

6.12 Candidate Preferences

While you were developing the position description, candidates were considering what they liked and disliked in their current environment and developing ideas about what they wanted in a new position. It is beneficial to all when these preferences are discussed openly at the interview. Be sure to discuss those of particular importance to your organization with each candidate.

6.12.1 Technologies System administrators have preferences for particular technologies. These include both hardware and software technologies. Some are interested in the integration of various unusual hardware components, while others prefer developing new software solutions for day-to-day tasks. The set of tools with which system administrators are comfortable and competent will indicate their technology preferences. Some system administrators are early adopters and switch to new systems easily. Others are comfortable using existing or older tools until they can no longer solve the problems faced. The comfort level in adopting new tools and integrating use into a daily tool box differs with each system administrator.

If you are looking for new solutions to the mail delivery scheme for your organization, you might ask:

- Have the candidates explored a variety of mail delivery agents? If so, which ones?
- What kinds of experiences have they had with mailers?
- What did they like or dislike?
- What was each system good at? Bad at?

Similar questions can be developed to learn about any tools candidates use.

6.12.2 Time Commitment The time commitment staff members make to their job can be a serious issue. Candidates will have an idea about how much time they are willing to give to an employer and frequently come with questions prepared. Questions candidates might ask include:

- What is the standard time commitment? (daily/weekly)
- Is a pager required?
- If so, what is the frequency? Rotating? 7x24?
- Is there direct compensation for carrying a pager?
- Is compensatory time given for hours worked outside of the regular work day/week?
- Is flex time an option?
- Is telecommuting an option?
- Is home equipment provided by the employer, or by the employee?

Based on your production schedule, there may be other special time-related issues. For example, there may be times during the year when the workload is very high or very low. Discussing these times at the interview can help candidates better understand the environment of your organization, and set expectations of the job.

6.12.3 *Workload* Sometimes projects demand extra time and effort for days or weeks. Some individuals prefer one project of this type per month, others only one per year. At other times, a standard routine of installation, upgrades, and general administration tasks may be the norm for weeks or months. Some individuals prefer the routine aspects of system administration. Others like to be faced with a challenge every day. It is a mismatch in workload to assign maintenance tasks of adding user accounts and updating mail aliases to a candidate who was looking for an exciting career in system integration and administration. Variation between regular maintenance and stressful situations of project implementation and crisis resolution can either be attractive or unattractive to an applicant.

6.12.4 *Training Issues* Commitment to ongoing employee training is an indication to candidates that the organization is serious about keeping skills sharp. Candidates are likely to ask:

- How many technical conferences or workshops am I permitted to attend each year?
- How much company funding will be available for these events?
- What resources are available for self-study?
- What priority is placed on soft skills and what kinds of training is appropriate or required in these areas?

Deciding how much training an employee will need after joining the organization is an issue separate from the training the employee desires. Consider the following:

- Are there tools or products used at your organization that a new employee will need to learn?
- Are there conventions for project tracking or time management about which the candidate will need detailed instruction?

6.12.5 Travel Some individuals like to travel, others don't. Understanding the travel commitment and being realistic about the frequency of travel is beneficial. Be honest about the travel commitment in the position you are filling. A candidate may be willing and able to travel one week a quarter or only one week a year. Another candidate might be prefer to travel one week a month but not two.

Traveling with little or no notice can be an issue for an individual with personal commitments. You cannot ask questions directly about these commitments, but you need to make the travel needs known. Use questions such as:

- This job requires traveling [some frequency]. Do you know of anything that would prevent you from fulfilling this requirement?
- This job requires traveling with little or no notice. Can you think of anything that might cause this to be a problem for you?

Hiring an individual who hasn't traveled frequently into a position for which travel is required immediately can result in frustration by both parties. Travel can look glamorous at first, but some individuals find that it isn't all they expected. Ask candidates how frequently they have traveled in the past, and how frequently they prefer to travel.

6.12.6 Candidate Relocation If a candidate will be relocating to join your organization, there can be other auxiliary considerations, including, but not limited to spouse, children, parents, pets, housing and local schools. Information about matters like housing, tax rates, school districts, transportation, services and attractions can help the candidate in making a decision. If this kind of information is available to the candidates in a printed or Web-based format, they can in turn provide it to others who are involved in the decision-making process. Relocation expenses and the timing of a start date are issues that need to be settled in the negotiation of the offer.

6.13 When a Good Candidate Doesn't Exactly Fit the Job

Sometimes a good candidate appears who doesn't exactly fit the open position. Deciding on such a candidate can be either easy or difficult. If you have a specific need that must be filled, there is little choice but to turn down good candidates who do not precisely meet the position requirements. Hiring such individuals can entail high training costs, long start-up time, or not knowing exactly where to place the new employee. On the other hand, sometimes an applicant is so outstanding in technical skills, interpersonal skills, or range of experience that you want to tailor a position for this individual. Making the decision to select an individual who doesn't exactly match the available position is ultimately dependent on being able to fill the need that was originally identified.

6.13.1 Inexperienced but Bright It can be preferable to choose a candidate who knows 50% of the material required on the first day and is highly motivated and bright, over an individual who knows more but doesn't appear to have the ability or desire to dig in and start right up. The investment in training a new employee can be highly beneficial, because the opportunity is available to provide training for precisely the skills needed. In smaller organizations, this is often less feasible, because during the training period, less of the day-to-day work can be accomplished. An inexperienced individual sometimes requires placement in a position where mistakes are more easily tolerated or absorbed – for example, installing new equipment, rather than maintaining production or mission-critical systems. In an environment where there is significant change and new technology exploration, an individual who is inexperienced, but bright and motivated, can be a better choice than an experienced individual who is less flexible or slower in learning new skills.

6.13.2 Experienced but High-Priced Sometimes a candidate is identified who is everything described in the job posting and more. Generally such candidates command high salaries. If a high-level system administrator position was targeted, appropriate funds should have been budgeted ahead of time to anticipate the need for high salary dollars. If an unexpectedly good candidate becomes available, salary can be an issue. Deciding to select such a candidate can introduce both good and potentially controversial issues into the work group. For example:

- Does the salary demand fit within the general bounds of what is able to be offered?
- How does the salary need compare to other comparable staff?
- How many additional skills will this individual bring as a side effect of being experienced?
- How will these skills enhance the performance of existing staff?
- How might they detract from the current skill pool?

Sometimes an excellent candidate cannot be hired because salary justifications cannot be made. Sometimes excellent candidates are selected because they can bring advanced skills to the organization. Be prepared ahead of time to deal with an unexpectedly fine candidate and be aware of the issues raised in such a circumstance.

6.14 Checking References

Checking a candidate's references might be handled by the HR department or it may be something in which the hiring manager wants to participate directly. Some organizations check references before interviewing a candidate; others wait until the first personal interview is completed, and then only check references of final candidates. References are a valuable source for input on a candidate's technical skills and work habits. Always make sure that a reference list is obtained by the end of the first interview, including information about how to contact each reference and the relationship of the candidate to the reference.

Keeping a distinct record for each reference called eliminates confusion when references are reviewed with the interview team at a later time. When the call is made, make sure it is a convenient time for the reference and clearly identify yourself and the name of the candidate about whom you are speaking. Appendix D contains some sample questions to ask references.

7.0 Expectations

The hiring process can range from being an exciting, invigorating step in the development of a system administration team to a tiring, discouraging effort to locate someone to do a job. Setting and maintaining appropriate expectations can lead to more of the former and less of the latter. Understanding the local economy, your organization's hiring process, skills required, the salary you can afford to offer, and what you hope to achieve in hiring new staff will help set appropriate expectations. Ideal candidates rarely materialize on the doorstep; it is best not to expect that they will. Don't set expectations too low and accept a candidate who doesn't meet the needs originally identified. Building a reputation in the local system administration community for your organization can help attract excellent candidates.

7.1 Your Expectations

Maintaining a good attitude throughout the hiring process can be difficult. There are high points and low points in any organization's process. In a large organization, frustrations can occur waiting for appropriate paperwork to clear from one department to another. In a small company, attracting candidates can be challenging because of a lack of general resources.

Understanding the environment and available resources will help set your expectations so the process is profitable and ends with the hiring of a qualified candidate. If a hiring process generally takes ten weeks in your organization, expecting to complete the process in less time can result in disappointment. Expecting to attract several excellently qualified candidates who are all willing to accept a position may also result in disappointment. If your organization has one system administration position open, realistically only one qualified and willing candidate needs to be identified. If two qualified candidates happen to be available, and you are able to choose between them, this is a situation beyond your minimum need.

7.2 Your Supervisor's and Organization's Expectations

System administration can be a mysterious profession. If your organization hasn't needed system administrators in the past, helping your supervisor and organization understand the basic facets of system administration will help them better understand what kind of person is needed and why. If your organization has a long history of system administration, it is still beneficial for your supervisor to understand the various issues encountered in any particular hiring cycle.

Using salary surveys can help set the expectations about reasonable salaries in your area. If funding is available to hire someone who performs SAGE Level 2 tasks in your area, expecting to hire a SAGE Level 4 is unreasonable, unless other benefits can take the place of salary money, such as additional time off, flexibility, and stock options.

7.3 The Candidate's Expectations

Part of the hiring process includes providing each candidate with an appropriate view of your organization. Candidates who have an accurate view of your organization can make an informed decision about joining your team. A hiring process is wasted if a candidate accepts a job and quits soon after starting because too little was known about the organization before accepting the job.

Candidates will have questions about many aspects of the job, including types of tasks to be handled, work environment, hours, travel, training, and benefits. Having answers to these questions available at the interview will help set each candidate's expectations of your organization. Including a system administrator on the interview team will allow candidates a chance to ask questions of someone who is in a similar position.

7.3.1 Introduce Candidates to the Work Environment If possible, include a brief walk-through of your facilities on the interview. Let candidates see the machine room, offices, and other resources available to them, such as libraries, conference areas, and lounges. This can help candidates better understand the work environment. The more the candidates know about your organization, the better equipped they will be to make an informed decision about accepting or declining an offer.

8.0 Making the Offer

Once an appropriate candidate is identified, an offer is made. All offers should be made in writing and include complete details of salary, benefits, and a basic review of the job description. A verbal offer may not be considered seriously by a candidate without a subsequent written offer. Additionally, failure to make an offer in a timely fashion can result in losing a good candidate. System administrators are in high demand; waiting to make an offer can result in a candidate no longer being available. Be familiar with the procedure your organization uses for making offers. The following questions should be considered:

- Does the HR department make the offer?
- Is the hiring manager or selection committee responsible for making the offer?
- To whom should the candidate respond?
- Who is responsible for handling any negotiation on salary or benefits?

8.1 Negotiating

Negotiation of the final offer is not an uncommon part of the hiring process. Knowing what issues can arise and how they can be addressed will help present a thoughtful, well organized view of your organization to candidates before they become employees. Some part of the negotiation will be with the candidate; however before you can negotiate with the candidate, you need to be aware of the flexibility that you have, which may mean negotiating within your organization.

8.2 Negotiating with Your Organization

Some organizations have great flexibility in the salary range and benefits offered to candidates. Other organizations have only minimal flexibility. Before you prepare an offer letter, understand how far your organization is willing and able to go to secure the best candidate. Understanding the value placed on a position will help make resources available for it. Deciding what trade-offs can be made within your own area will insure that the best candidate is selected and appropriately compensated for the position.

8.3 Negotiating with the Candidate

Sometimes a candidate accepts a job on the first offer. Sometimes additional clarification is needed, and then the initial offer is accepted. Sometimes the initial offer is not acceptable and the candidate indicates the areas needing negotiation, such as salary, start date, and benefits. Knowing what your organization is willing and able to give allows the negotiations with the candidate to go smoothly.

9.0 SAGE Community Thoughts

Some members of the SAGE community were kind enough to relate experiences with hiring and training system administrators. Their comments are collected here as a series of answers to various questions.

9.1 Inexperienced System Administrators

9.1.1 *Have you ever hired an inexperienced but bright system administrator?*

We have hired inexperienced folks for our install/configure team. Most of them have limited experience with systems administration. For the everyday, repetitive procedure-driven stuff, this seems to work well.

As a part of the University system administrator training program, I was often hiring student administrators who had more enthusiasm than experience. I have paid a price when I tried to do the same thing as a small business. So at the University, I was able to afford the costs associated with inexperienced sysadmins. In a small business, I am finding the costs too high.

I think using inexperienced staff is the way to find the talented system administrators. Suppose someone just graduated from the University, and he is not employed just because he has no experience. Hiring inexperienced administrators is a way to provide experience. It is how we develop our own community.

I think that the break-even falls out of how many slough tasks you have. If you have places like system installations or rote work that you can give inexperienced people as training grounds, then you can afford to hire them and train them. But if you only have a few system administrators and they have to be on their feet to solve diverse problems, then you can't afford inexperience.

9.1.2 *What made you select an inexperienced person?*

If we are getting clobbered by low-end tasks like machine installations, we try not to busy out the more experienced people with these tasks. We try to fit the type of person we need to the workload we need to address.

I always look for enthusiasm as a starting point. Someone who is actively setting up systems and actively trying new things.

We have younger staff move into our more developed positions, and try to concentrate our recruiting only on low-end positions. This helps us in defining and developing exactly the skills we need at our site.

One time, I interviewed (and subsequently hired) someone who told me that she didn't know everything, or even a lot about what was needed for system administration, but she could learn anything and was willing to try. She can and I think she's great!

9.1.3 What training did you provide?

We have a combination of senior folks, staff at the same level, and documentation to address the training issues. Sometimes it works smoothly; other times we have people going off the map and we have to reel them in.

We have the junior staff attend our meetings on a regular basis to get a sense of what is happening on the site, what our concerns are. They also get to voice their issues to us, which can be just as important.

We use two models. We provide direct training by having them attend a system administration course. We also have a hands-on apprenticeship program. I think that you really need both.

I always put people in a place where they can safely fail. Then over time they can grow into more responsibilities. I carefully select tasks that are safe for them to fail at.

Breaking down projects into smaller tasks can be helpful to a less experienced staff member. Years ago, I was asked to set up a network server. I was scared to death, but when the job was described in simple steps – "install OS, configure OS, install the applications, . . ." – I was able to accomplish the project easily.

9.1.4 What did you find to be the pros and cons?

Inexperienced people can fall into large holes very quickly despite the best prep. There is also the gamble that once they are involved, it is not what they really wanted to do. (This job requires a certain temperament and if you don't have it, you are not going to do well or be engaged.) We have had inexperienced folks who have absorbed everything we throw at them and take advantage of the opportunity. We have had inexperienced people who only learned how to surf the Net. The latter do not survive long here. If you get the right people and give them the spark, you can build them into what your organization specifically needs. That is the classic use of inexperienced folks: to imprint them with YOUR experience.

Enthusiasm wins over everything, except for people whose enthusiasm overrides their planning and discipline.

9.2 Experienced System Administrators

9.2.1 Have you ever hired a very experienced system administrator?

Hiring senior staff is the hardest, most time-consuming employment effort we expend. It has the potential for the biggest payoff.

In our small company, we can't afford to train someone on all the basics. We can teach them about our local environment but we need someone who knows the material on the day they start. For us, we can't afford to hire anything but experienced.

We recently hired an experienced system administrator from local industry and found that he brought us more experience and perspective than we could have ever imagined.

9.2.2 What made you select an experienced person?

Our environment keeps getting more complex and demanding. When we see a hole in our organization, we try to identify it and find someone who can fill it. We also benefit from folks who have worked in a variety of environments where the implementations differ from ours.

When we are in need of someone who can step in and start working right away, we spend the time to find an experienced candidate. Training someone, allowing training time, and then finding start-up projects sometimes just takes too long on projects with time-critical constraints.

We generally hire young staff and train them ourselves, but we were beginning to feel a bit inbred. We felt that finding someone with a different experience background would increase the variety of our expertise.

9.2.3 How did they fit with your existing organization?

One of the things we try to screen for is compatibility with the existing team. We have had some folks with the skill set but not the temperament to work with us. We look for team players, people we would not mind spending hours/days/years with us. Because they will.

In spite of our laid-back environment, it took an experienced person longer than expected to fit into the group and get used to the university setting. Mostly, he had to find his niche in the group and it took longer than we expected. This was actually an interesting lesson, because we expected the integration to be much smoother. However, the final result was worth the wait.

9.2.4 What training did you provide?

Senior staff, by definition, require a lot less training. There are orientation issues and the local conventions to pass along. Most senior folks pick up on where things are very quickly. Our training generally involves working on joint projects with the new team member. We generally have our staff two to an office, so there is a natural pairing and mentoring with your office mate.

We track the work of new team members to make certain there are no mis-steps. They still happen, but we like to keep everyone included in the early stages.

We have an employee orientation program that covers not only an introduction to our organization, but also a variety of documentation about how we perform our system administration tasks. This includes things from how we do our backups, to why we use various security programs, and how to install them on your workstation to make it usable in our environment.

All new staff members are paired with someone in the group who is responsible for making sure that the new person has someone to ask (besides the manager) for various problems or questions.

9.2.5 What did you find to be the pros and cons of hiring an experienced person?

A senior staff member can be a mentor for the team as well as for an individual. New people shake us out of our current thinking and ways of doing things. The energy can be quite revitalizing for the existing team. We are constantly learning in this profession. Senior staff carry the weight for keeping the enthusiasm and the technology where they need to be. New members can add a spark.

The cons can be a senior member who is less open or sharing, who wants to be a local guru and is less interested in teamwork. This profession generates strong team players and egomaniac godheads. The latter can be brilliant but are mostly unusable in the day-to-day work situation. Even if their technology is correct, the application to the environment may be misplaced, because there is no consideration of the user community or how this technology will interact with what is already established. If the staff member forgets he is part of a *service* organization, the value he brings to the team is greatly diminished.

Another look at the team issue is how senior staff share expertise. If they are shamed because a problem stumps them, they are less likely to ask a second time and things can go unfixed. If the senior staff can unabashedly admit they do not know how a certain tool or procedure works, trusting that their peer will help them out, you have a healthy team. If this same individual is met with scorn, not only do they not ask a second time, they might withhold assistance from their peer when he/she is in a similar quandary.

Smoothing the ruffled feathers of existing staff was a problem for us when a new experienced staff member was hired. He asked intelligent questions about many of our procedures that made us rethink how we do things day-to-day. Many we didn't change but some we did. Introducing a new thought process was a challenge for us.

9.3 Candidate Evaluations

9.3.1 What is your basic technique for evaluating candidates?

We use a phone screen and then a group interview. The group interview will include a range of technical skill questions and interpersonal situations to see how the candidate responds. We try to keep the interview challenging but not threatening for the candidate. While we want to see how a person responds to pressure, we do not feel we have license for abuse.

Our HR department ranks the candidates based upon the job description we provided. They then pass all the resumes to the hiring manager. Also, HR participates in the selection of the interview team. After passing a telephone interview candidates then have individual interviews with each team member.

The hiring manager receives the resumes and phone screens the candidates. The resumes of the candidates seem OK on the phone interview are passed around and we decide whether or not to bring the candidate in for a written test. Then we grade the test and, based on the test and phone screen result, decide whether to bring the candidate in for a formal panel interview. A panel interview usually consists of 6 to 10 individuals (staff members in our group and customer representatives) in a room and each asks questions. We distribute the written test results and resumes to the panel members before the personal interviews.

9.3.2 How much do soft skills count?

If soft skills means the ability to interact well with other humans, they count significantly.

If the candidate demonstrates a lack of interest in the customer or displays any "godlike" tendencies, this does not bode well for them.

If the candidate demonstrates an understanding of what it means to be in a support organization, we respond favorably, it means less training for us. And some things can't really be taught.

There are some things we will forgive. A strong accent or incomplete grasp of English is given some latitude if there is not a major communication issue, especially if the technical skills are superior and the candidate shows a strong desire to assist users. Since part of the job is clear communication with the user, we cannot dismiss this concern. We don't like to disqualify folks solely on this basis.

9.3.3 How do you evaluate soft/technical skills?

Most of this is intuitive. Sometimes the candidate makes an obvious gaffe, but more often when we get to the "touchy-feely" part of an evaluation, one has to go with gut impressions.

We are particularly interested in how people manage their time and their projects. We ask questions about organization techniques and how they would handle competing problems or projects.

At the personal interview, we may ask technical questions if we are unsure of the candidate's technical skill level. One of my favorite questions is to ask candidates to write on the white board in 3 languages (C, any shell, and PERL) a short program to print "hello world" infinitely many times. I like this question because it is simple, and if a candidate can write things close enough, that's good enough for me. However, we can also use this to screen out candidate who claimed to have a lot of development experience but cannot write the simplest form of program.

Our managers like to ask situation questions. Like how would you handle the following situation (customer related, work related etc.). We also asked the candidate to ask us questions.

9.3.4 Do you use a skills matrix?

No. I think that such a device has the illusion of objectifying the subjective. I would sooner have the group's gut feelings stated as such. Although there are organized procedures for conducting and evaluating a candidate, this instrument is suspect for me. If an interviewer is having a bad day and they give a candidate a "2," it doesn't really reflect on the candidate. Also, the interviewer may even feel the score must be defended once it is written down.

We use a simple yes/no scheme. The candidate with the most yes slots ranks the highest. We include both technical and people skills in this ranking.

Not really. Immediately after the candidate has left the personal interview, each panel member gives their opinion in the form of a score between 1 and 5 for the candidate. The manager will then take all the information and make the decision.

9.3.5 Do you give a test (written or verbal)?

We give a lengthy written examination with the intention of determining the limits of each applicant's knowledge base. The questions range from simple conceptual discussions to actual problem solving situations.

Our written test consists of 2 parts, a system administration section and a programming section. The test was designed to be completed in an hour. The goal is to test the basic skills of a candidate. We tell the candidates that they do not have to get it completely right, we are more interested in the skills the candidates have. We expect candidates to have some system administration knowledge, some database knowledge, some programming skills. Other tests have more system administration–specific questions, like backup and recovery, file system format, network, etc.

Our interview is a verbal exam. None have died. A few wish they had . . . :)

9.3.6 What kinds of things do you always evaluate?

UNIX competency. Awareness of networking concepts and procedures. Hardware configuration knowledge. Scripting and programming preferences and strengths. Trouble-shooting skills.

We always have some diagnostic problems that are open-ended, so that we can see how the candidate approaches problem solving. The idea is not that they get the "right" answer. The idea is to see how many ways they can skin that damned cat. We've all been in this situation and our attempts to simulate it have been pretty revealing. To be fair, we tell the candidate up front we are looking for this.

We always look for networking competencies. Our business is highly network based and all candidates must have a complete grasp of networking protocols and tools.

We look for a combination of programming and system administration skills. Since we are a development shop, even our system administrators should have basic programming skills.

I always look for how the person will fit into our existing group. If the person is bright and can learn new things, that is what is important to our group.

Appendix A: Advertisements

Advertisements range from being very bad to very good. The variety within bad advertisements is large. It is easy to design an advertisement that looks good but produces bad results. By following the guidelines described in Chapter 3, you can develop an effective advertisement.

Bad Advertisement — Laundry List

A particularly bad advertisement is one that includes a laundry list of required skills with little or no information about the organization or the benefits that an applicant can expect to receive.

Our systems administration team has an opening for a senior systems administrator with broad background in heterogeneous system and network administration (SUN, IRIX, AIX, Windows NT, routers). Working with one junior SA the responsibilities include strategic tasks such as:

Systems architecture development and integration
Planning and development of a wide area Intranet
Responsibility for companywide Internet connection
Vendor contracts and relations; equipment planning and ordering

as well as technical expertise with:

DHCP, DNS, IPX, NIS+, PERL, TCP/IP, RAID management, sendmail configuration
Multi-vendor UNIX system administration tools
UNIX and Windows desktop and server system administration
Oracle and Informix database administration tasks
Web server installation and maintenance
Development of in-house IS tools and applications
Third-party application installation and maintenance

The successful applicant will have:

> Significant experience with UNIX environments & utilities
> Experience with many flavors of UNIX administration
> Experience with Windows 95 and Windows NT administration
> Experience with TCP/IP and IPX LAN administration
> Experience with Web server administration
> Excellent communication skills
> BS/MS degree in Computer Science or Engineering preferred

Benefit package commensurate with experience. To apply for this position, please fax or email a resume and a cover letter highlighting your interests and skills. Please fax resumes to 555-POOR-ADS Attn: Recruiting, or send by email (PostScript, or MS Word only) to jobs@poor-ads.com. Please refer to this posting.

The preceding advertisement gives no information about the size of the community supported, the number of machines or users, or the distribution of the machines. Is there one each of these various types of machines or are there several hundred? Is the Internet connection already in place or will the new employee be responsible for establishing it? There is no unique identifier, such as reference ID or position posting number, so it is be difficult for applicants to refer to the specific posting.

Bad Advertisement – Too Short
Some advertisements give too little information about both the requirements and the company. These make it appear as if the organization is not serious about the recruitment process.

> Wanted: UNIX Sys Admin in Palo Alto. Solaris and NIS experience a must. Fax resume to (800)POOR-ADS or email to jobs@poor-ads.com.

Good Advertisement
A good advertisement includes information about your organization, a clear description of the skills both preferred and required, and complete information about how to apply for the position.

> GoodPlace Inc. (located in NiceWeather, US) is seeking candidates for the position of Intermediate/Advanced UNIX Systems Administrator. Be part of a team providing infrastructure support to developers, engineers and sales staff.
>
> > 4+ years of full time experience with Solaris (other versions of UNIX a plus)
> > Hands-on expertise in NFS, DNS, NIS, sendmail and SCCS
> > Knowledge of both networking hardware (hubs, routers) and protocols (TCP/IP)

Familiarity with system/network security including TCPD, SSH and firewalls concepts
Strong communications and interpersonal skills

For additional information see: http://goodplace/jobs/unix.html.
All applications should reference the reply code USA-GOOD1.
Please FAX your resume to (800) GOOD-ADS or email ASCII or PostScript to
jobs@goodplace.org. Paper resumes can be sent to:
Recruitment
GoodPlace Inc.
1000 Perfect Street
NiceWeather, US.

Appendix B: Evaluation Tool

Once the position description is complete, turn it into a definite list of requirements for the job. For example, the following list was for a UNIX system administrator at a medium-sized university.

Candidate Name	
Interview Date	
Rating (Y/N) (1-5)	
	Resume indicated candidate had:
	a. Formal education preferred
	b. Applicable work experience
	c. Adequate programming and/or design experience
	d. Up-to-date skills
	e. Consulting experience
	f. Training experience
	g. Documentation experience
	Able to work full-time
	Interested in a permanent position
	Has preferred degree
	Has necessary writing skills
	Has necessary verbal skills
	Demonstrated experience in one/many of the following:
	a. Networking – TCP/IP / IPX
	b. X11
	c. UNIX
	d. General hardware exposure
	e. Teaching
	f. Perl
	g. C programming
	h. AIX – IRIX – Solaris – Linux
	i. NFS or DFS
	k. DNS
	Leadership, public speaking, self-confidence necessary
	Displayed growth potential
	Salary requirement reasonable
	Interested in job after being interviewed
	Discussion with previous employer indicated no limitations
	References gave a positive appraisal

If a position description is not available to turn into a skill summary, it is possible to use a general template with various skill areas outlined:

Candidate Name	
Interview Date	
Rating (Y/N) (1-5)	
	Technical skills:
	System installation
	Application installation
	Application development
	Systems integration
	Operating systems:
	UNIX
	NT
	Windows95/98
	VMS
	Other
	Programming skills:
	Shell programming (csh/ksh/sh)
	Perl
	Awk/sed/grep
	C programming
	Networking skills:
	TCP/IP
	IPX
	Appletalk
	Window systems:
	X11
	OpenWindows
	CDE
	Interpersonal skills:
	Conflict resolution
	Negotiation
	Eye contact
	Self-confidence
	Work style:
	Interests
	Focus
	Other

Appendix C: Interview Questions

Telephone Interview

The phone interview is a time to get to know a little bit about each candidate who submitted a resume or application and is minimally qualified. This group can be anywhere from 10% to 50% of the applications received. The phone interview step helps in learning information about the applicant that isn't necessarily available on the resume. Make sure the applicant's materials are available before you begin the phone interview. You can review the application materials with the applicant if clarification of any items is necessary.

Telephone interviews are best held outside of normal working hours. If candidates indicated a best time to call on their application or resume, by all means use it. If there is difficulty reaching a candidate, leaving a message is appropriate. On an answering machine, you can leave a message such as:

> *This is YOUR NAME calling from YOUR ORGANIZATION about a possible employment opportunity. Please call me at YOUR NUMBER between TIME1 and TIME2 or send me e-mail at YOUR@NET.ADDRESS. Thank you.*

This message does not give any indication that the individual you called applied for a position and does give them enough information to contact you.

The goal of the phone interview is to determine if an applicant is a viable candidate for a personal interview. Information you should try to discover during the phone interview includes:

- What interests the candidate in your organization?
- What kinds of experience does the candidate have?
- What are some of his/her skills?
- How do they describe the job of system administration?
- Does their view fit with what your needs are?
- What does their work style preference appear to be?
- Can they be directed in conversation?

Once you have connected with applicants, give your full attention and begin by identifying yourself:

This is YOUR NAME calling from YOUR ORGANIZATION about your application for the VACANCY position.

Then make sure it is a good time to talk, or arrange a time when it is convenient. Phone interviews must often be conducted in the evening, so careful planning of the phone interview is important. The phone interview time can be arranged by electronic mail if the applicant has provided an email address.

Would you have a few minutes to talk now?

Can we arrange a time to talk?

Next, giving a brief introduction to your organization and the available position will give the applicant some framework in which to answer the questions. An introduction such as:

As you may know, YOUR ORGANIZATION produces TYPE OF WORK or PRODUCT. Our group of system administrators has N members and provides support for Y users and Z workstations of types A, B & C.

It can be appropriate to provide other brief information about your organization or group now, or this can be held for later, when the applicant has questions.

Next give a brief description of your objective for the phone interview.

We are conducting telephone interviews with some applicants for the open position of POSITION to narrow the field to those with whom we will conduct personal interviews.

Finally, begin with your telephone interview questions.

Why are you interested in working at YOUR ORGANIZATION rather than SOME OTHER?

For example:

Why are you interested in working at a university rather than in industry?

or

I see you are working at a large company now, what attracts you to our small start-up?

This will give some idea of how the applicant sees your organization and can give insight about the kinds of work in which the applicant is interested. Answers often include discussion of management styles, resources, workload, and many other things. Noting the reasons given will provide for customized follow-up in other questions.

What kinds of experience do you have?

This can help you discover not how much experience an applicant has but the type of experience. If you are told how many years of experience or how many workstations the applicant has installed, you can then follow up with the following questions:

For those N workstations, what exactly was your responsibility?

What kinds of support did you provide?

Over those N years, what different responsibilities did you have?

What kinds of situations did you encounter?

This will give another opportunity to discuss the variety and exact tasks that have been encountered in the past. You can probe various basic skills, based upon the level of the available position and the candidate's past experience.

Which versions of UNIX have you installed? Solaris? AIX? Linux? What did you find the most difficult about each?

Have you installed application software on Solaris? AIX? Linux? Which packages? Did you find anything particularly interesting or challenging in installing these? If so, what?

Questions that give applicants the opportunity to tell about what they did and what they found difficult give special insight. Knowing what applicants find difficult and how they overcame those difficulties will help you determine how they will fit into your organization. Applicants who find configuring the print system on a machine difficult until they discover the GUI tool may be at a different skill level than applicants who find it difficult to develop the serial driver for a custom piece of hardware. Since the question asks what was difficult for them, it allows them the opportunity to be honest without being afraid of making a mistake. To gain additional information, follow up questions about difficult problems by asking how they resolved the difficulty. If the users of GUI tools explain how they looked at the files that the GUI touched and figured out how to manipulate the files by hand, this adds to your understanding of what they consider a complete learning and resolution process.

Have you consulted with others on using applications, or helped others resolve their problems? What applications?

Tell me about a difficult question with which you helped someone else. Why was it hard for them and what was hard for you in answering their question?

These questions can help understand applicants' ability to work with others who have less developed technical skills. They also help to determine an applicant's skill level based upon the difficulty of the problem. If others consult with the applicant about the pros and cons of various mailers like sendmail or qmail, that individual has a different skill set than someone who has helped others with the configuration of mail application defaults such as a *.pinerc* file.

Tell me about your familiarity with operational details of Solaris/AIX/ . . .

You will need to customize this question to your own environment. Consider the day-to-day knowledge that system administrators in your organization need to have, and ask the applicants to discuss these at a general level. In some organizations, staff may be performing routine system administration tasks such as maintaining usernames, group files and aliases, and system backups, yet don't understand the difference between the shell and the kernel. Asking applicants to discuss what they do know lets them discuss areas in which they are comfortable. It also gives the interviewer an opportunity to see where that level would fit in the organization without making the applicant feel uncomfortable.

Are you familiar with netstat? Can you describe what it does?

Questions like this can be developed in many areas. With this question, several answers can be considered correct. The first demonstrates that the applicant knows something about networking. They might answer, "Provides information on the status of current network connections, both TCP and UDP." In this case, you can continue with fundamental questions in other areas. A second correct answer is, "Has something to do with network status?" At least this applicant is able to analyze a word from its parts. The applicant may not have the desired technical skills, but could be useful in related capacities, or could be trainable if other technical questions turn out better. A third acceptable answer is, "I don't know." This is, of course, a correct answer, and can lead to asking more general questions to determine what the individual does know.

What is the Internet?

What's the difference between the World Wide Web and the Internet?

How does PPP work?

It is surprising how many people think they know something about the Internet but when asked can't explain anything more than "it's a complicated network of computers." If applicants give a reasonable answer about the Internet, asking them to explain the difference between it and the Web can help clarify their understanding. Asking about PPP can give an indication of the level of knowledge of networking protocols without scaring them, since PPP is a common tool that can be configured with little expertise.

If networking is a focus of the job, additional questions about subnets, netmasks and broadcast addresses can be asked. If hardware support is involved, questions about the differences among hubs, bridges, and routers are productive in determining the exact level of an applicant's expertise.

What is license service? Can you describe some different license service models?

Since license service, like netstat, has a relatively straightforward name, even applicants who haven't used it directly can venture a guess at what it is. Their answers can be enlightening about how they think computers work. Some applicants can give a good description about the difference between node-locked and floating licenses and the pros and cons of each. Some may give a vague answer about computers talking to each other, and others will know nothing about it.

Tell me about your favorite UNIX tool. Why is it your favorite?

If an applicant can't come up with something immediately, give a little hint by saying something such as: *"I like SCCS because . . . what do you like?"* This will give some insight into what kinds of productivity tools are used or how free time is spent. Recently, I've had to rephrase this question to say, *"Other than Netscape, what is your favorite UNIX tool?"* because it seems that all anyone ever does these days is surf the Web.

In your day-to-day tasks what editor do you use?

How do you read your mail?

If you were going to prepare a memo what text processor would you use? What about your resume?

When you use X (or equivalent), what window manager do you use? Which features do you like best about it?

These questions help determine organizational fit with your current staff and the work environment available, and some work habits of the applicant. Some of this will reflect the environment in which applicant has previously worked and the resources that were available. These questions don't have right or wrong answers; rather, they collect information about how applicants perform day-to-day tasks such as reading mail. Understanding what tools applicants use and are comfortable with will help determine if they complement existing staff skills, or if they will add additional depth to the existing skill set.

In your view, what are the biggest differences between A and B?

This question can be tailored to focus on the job or the applicant. If an applicant has both AIX and Solaris experience, the question can be phrased to ask for the differences between those two. Answers can range from a description involving user administration tools, to default shells, to filesystem implementation differences. The level at which applicants answer this question can give insight into their level of familiarity with the details of systems.

Similarly, the question can be tailored for databases by asking candidates with experience with Oracle and Sybase to explain some of the differences between them at a level at which they are comfortable. If they have done installations, ask a question such as:

What did you find to be the biggest difference between installing Oracle and installing Sybase?

or

What did you find the most difficult part of installing each database system with which you have worked?

This kind of question is particularly useful because it can probe into areas where the interviewer may not have expertise. If applicants' resumes say they have NIS+ experience and the interviewer only has knowledge of NIS, a question about how slaves and masters work in NIS+ is appropriate. It is a way to discover how well an applicant can explain a system or tool to someone who is familiar with the concepts but not familiar with the details. Again, this allows an applicant to answer at a level at which they are comfortable.

Would you describe the concepts behind a client server model.

Because so much of computing has evolved into clients and servers, being able to describe this model will serve a system administrator in good stead. Again, there are various levels of correct answers, including complete descriptions of how a system works, to an example of a particular system, such as mail.

What would you say are the broad responsibilities of a system administrator?

What would you say are the broad responsibilities of a user support person?

Sometimes the job of a system administrator is blurred with the job of user support. Having applicants describe the responsibilities of each job will help the interviewer understand the perception that the applicant has of system administration. If the applicant has difficulty defining these responsibilities, the question can be rephrased as

What are three important tasks for which a system administrator could be responsible?

This generally results in an answer such as, "Keep the systems running and respond to any problems." In turn you can ask,

What types of problems might an administrator be responsible for resolving?
How could these problems be resolved?

Having applicants describe what is involved in user support will also help clarify where the applicant thinks the line lies between system administration and user support. This line varies from organization to organization and in some the distinction doesn't exist at all.

What personality traits would you say a system administrator needs? What personality traits would you say a person doing user support needs?

These questions let the applicant describe for the interviewer an ideal candidate. They may or may not describe the applicant's own personality. Answers might include that a system administrator needs excellent problem solving skills while a user support person needs patience. A user support person needs to be able to describe systems to users while a system administrator needs to have design skills. These questions help clarify the applicant's perception of system administration.

Of all the work you have done, where have you been most successful?

Giving an applicant the opportunity to talk freely about successful projects, events, or achievements can tell you about accomplishments and satisfaction. If an applicant has trouble coming up with a circumstance, additional direction can be given by allowing consideration of school successes for a recent graduate, or personal achievements in a local community activity. It also offers insight into what motivates applicants and what each considers personal success.

How would you describe the perfect job for you?

Since one goal of the hiring process is to match jobs to people, understanding what the applicant thinks is an ideal job will help in making that match. If an applicant hesitates, take the opportunity to explain that understanding what the candidate thinks is desirable in a job helps in matching candidates to available positions. Some applicants might not be able to describe a perfect job, others will describe a job in general terms, such as a job with flexibility and opportunities to learn new things. Occasionally, an applicant answers with a restatement of the job description presented at the beginning of the interview. Whatever the answer, indicate that this information helps in finding the right fit for all involved.

Telephone Interview - Conclusion

The conversation can be concluded by thanking the applicants. Let them know additional candidates are being interviewed by telephone and that they will hear within some specified time about any future personal interviews. For example: *I don't know yet if you will make the personal interview list because I still have to talk with other applicants. You can expect to hear something in the next couple of weeks.* It is also appropriate to ask if they have any questions at this time. One common question applicants have is to know how many applicants applied for the position. Either a ballpark number or a reply of "more than we can interview" is an appropriate answer.

Personal Interview

Once the applicants have been screened for basic skills, it is time for personal interviews. The personal interview can be used as a time to reconfirm the technical skills identified during the telephone interview. If you use a series of short individual interviews, one of the team can review some of the questions, or ask additional questions to probe in areas that need more investigation. If a group interview is held, general questions can be asked again so that the group has the benefit of understanding the applicant's background.

The following questions can help discover how candidates view their current job, how they organize their time, how they approach projects, and how they interact with others. Many of these questions have been developed or modified from the book *Hiring the Best* by Martin Yate.

How does your job relate to the overall goals of your department?

What aspects of your work do you consider most crucial?

What are the three most important responsibilities in your current job?

What would you change about your current job? (What do you like least?)

What do you like the best about your current job?

What kinds of things bother you most about your job?

What was the most important project you worked on at your current job?

These questions give a framework for the environments in which the candidates currently work. It gives candidates an opportunity to talk about what they do in their job, what responsibilities they have, and what they like and dislike about their current environment. If they say that they don't like constantly working with new users, and prefer to have a stable set of machines and clients that they support, then they may not be suitable for working in a university environment where the clientele change every year.

How necessary is it for you to be creative on your job?

What are the most repetitive tasks in your job? How do you handle them?

System administration has aspects of repetition, new environments, problem solving, and creativity. Someone who doesn't handle repetition well would be a poor selection for installation of dozens of workstations, while someone who prefers repetition would be the ideal type of candidate.

How important was communication and interaction with others on this job?

What was more important, written or oral communication?

What was the most difficult report/document you ever had to write?

What made this the most difficult report/document?

Looking back, how would you have improved it?

When have you convinced people verbally of an approach to a task? Give an example.

Communication skills are important for the completion of projects. These questions offer the opportunity for candidates to articulate how they have used their communication skills on various projects. Giving candidates opportunities to use their hindsight for imagining how they could have improved a project helps them articulate their own weaknesses in a nonthreatening way. Also, for many it may be the first time that they have thought about how a project could have been improved.

Tell me about a time when you had a project that required you to interact with different levels/departments within the company – people above and beneath you.

How did you do this?

What caused you the most problems in executing your tasks?

With whom were you most comfortable?

Give candidates an opportunity to talk about something that they have successfully accomplished in the past, and allow them to reflect on the difficult parts. Giving them the chance to talk about situations in which they are comfortable and uncomfortable will help in determining how they will fit in your organization. If the candidates are uncomfortable or unhappy working with people who have different skill sets, they might be unhappy supporting workstations used by administrative staff, but happy supporting workstations of developers or university faculty.

Tell me about a time when you came up with a new method or idea.

How did you get it implemented/approved?

Can you think of a time when another idea or project was rejected?

Why was it rejected and what did you do about it?

If candidates are successful in convincing others to try new things, knowing how they did it will be important.

- Did they go through established procedures to get it approved?
- Did they change or install something and not tell anyone until after it was working?
- Did they try it on their own environment, and then show others?

Knowing how candidates handle situations where their ideas were rejected or not implemented can give some insight into how they deal with stressful or controversial situations. If individuals have always had their ideas accepted, your organization might be the first to deal them a rejection. Coping with rejection can be difficult for both employee and manager, and should be considered as a potential issue in the hiring process.

How do you feel about your workload at your current position?

How did you divide your time among your major areas of responsibility?

How do you organize and plan for major projects?

Recall for me a project that you worked on and how you organized it.

How many projects are you comfortable working on at one time?

How do you decide which one to work on at any particular time?

How do you organize yourself for day-to-day activities?

Since system administrators must balance between the planning and implementing new systems, and the maintenance of existing systems, the management of these time blocks is important. Knowing whether a candidate sets aside time daily to work on planning and development projects or handles these projects only after all maintenance projects are completed helps you understand how that candidate will fit in your organization.

Some people are happy to work on five or seven projects at one time, and can make positive progress on all of them at once. Other people are single threaded and like to handle only one or two projects at a time. Knowing your organization's environment and typical work style helps in matching the right candidate to the position available.

Tell me about a time when an emergency caused you to reschedule your projects.

What do you do when you have many tasks or projects to accomplish in a short time span? How have you reacted?

What do you do when there is a decision to be made and no procedure exists?

These questions help in understanding how a candidate thinks and performs under pressure. It gives a candidate an opportunity to talk about a crisis situation and how it was handled.

- Did all other projects get dropped?
- Did they ask co-workers for help?
- Did they discuss workload with their supervisor?
- If they made a decision on their own, how did it work out?

If system administrators need to work independently most of the time, then selecting a candidate who can make decisions independently will have a superior outcome. If system administrators generally work in a team, then selecting a candidate who is comfortable with consulting others about workload and procedures will be better.

Do you set goals for yourself?

Do you always reach your goals?

Tell me about a time when you failed to reach a goal.

While not all system administrators are goal oriented, many are. Knowing what kinds of goals candidates set for themselves, and how they handle not reaching their goals, helps in understanding how they handle their workload and how they will fit in your organization. If a candidate maintains reaching all or most goals, discovering that candidate's techniques will be important.

- Do they ask for input from others?
- Do they use creative methods when at an impasse?
- Do they break the goal into subgoals?
- Do they use brute force?

Sometimes people finds themselves in situations where they wish they were better at something. Sometimes I wish I were better at <fill in your favorite here>. When you have been in difficult or crisis situations, which areas of your professional skills do you vow to work on further?

Tell me about self-improvement efforts you are currently making in this area.

Nobody is perfect. Everyone has weaknesses, and everyone can work on improving some professional skill. Fill in the first part of the question with an example from your own experience, and then give candidates an opportunity to talk about where they would like to improve and where they find their own weaknesses.

Are you prepared to work non-traditional hours?

Can you think of anything that would prevent you from handling unusual situations at unusual hours on short notice?

Are you prepared to perform duties that may not be a part of your regular routine?

Since system administration tasks don't necessarily conform to traditional work hours, these questions help understand a candidate's willingness and ability to work flexible hours. Additionally, sometimes a system administrator needs to be a jack of all trades. Configuring or moving hardware may not be a regular part of a job description, but it could be required in a crisis situation. Knowing if a candidate is willing and able to complete an entire job will help in selecting the best candidate.

Tell me about a time when your manager was in a rush and didn't have time for niceties.

What are some of the things about which you and your boss disagree?

What are some of the things about which you and your boss agree?

What are some of the things your boss did that you disliked?

What are some of the things your boss did that you liked?

In what areas could your boss have done a better job?

How does your boss get the best out of you?

How do you get the best out of your boss?

Would you like to have your boss's job?

If you could make one constructive suggestion to management, what would it be?

How an employee interacts with his/her supervisor is an important part of a job. If a candidate has left a job over a disagreement with a supervisor, find out the subject of that disagreement, what compromise or negotiations took place in an effort to resolve the conflict, and why the candidate thought leaving was the only solution. Remember to reassure candidates that anything they share about their supervisors will be held in confidence.

Personal Interview Closing

The following questions from *Hiring the Best*, by Martin Yate, make an excellent set of closing questions which allow the interviewer and the candidates to come to a common understanding about how the candidates view the position and their potential contributions.

1. *Are you interested in the job?*

2. *What interests you most about it?*

3. *What interests you least?*

4. *How long will it take you to make a contribution?*

5. *Should you be offered the job, how long will it take you to make a decision?*

6. *Why should I offer you the job?*

7. *What can you do for us that someone else cannot do?*

8. *What special characteristics should I consider about you as a person when considering you for this job?*

Finally, close the interview by offering the candidate a final opportunity to discuss anything that was not covered.

Is there anything else you want to tell me or do you have any other questions that I can answer for you?

Appendix D: Reference Questions

As with the telephone interview, it is important to make sure you clearly identify yourself, state the purpose of your telephone call and confirm a convenient time for the person you are calling.

May I speak to: REFERENCE NAME?

This is YOUR NAME calling from ORGANIZATION about CANDIDATE. At a recent job interview, HE/SHE has given your name as a reference.

9. *Would you have a few minutes to talk now?*
   Can we arrange a time to talk?

10. Give a brief description of the job:
    The job being filled is a system administration position with focus on UNIX support; it is highly technical with frequent/infrequent interaction with the user community.

11. *How long have you known PERSON?*

12. *What is your relationship with PERSON?*

13. *What was PERSON'S position and title?*
    When did PERSON start with your organization?
    What was PERSON's position/title?

14. *What would you characterize as PERSON's strongest interpersonal skill?*
    Weakest?

15. *Does PERSON work independently?*
    a) Does S/HE solve problems on HER/HIS own?
    b) Does S/HE independently research new areas?
    c) Does S/HE manage HER/HIS time thoughtfully?
    d) Does S/HE follow directions well?

16. *Does PERSON have a grasp of UNIX/Networking fundamentals?*
    How would you rate HIS/HER technical skills?
    a) What would you describe as HIS/HER strengths?
    b) What would you describe as HIS/HER weaknesses?

17. *Can PERSON clearly explain fundamental concepts to others?*
    How would you characterize HIS/HER written skills?
    How would you characterize HIS/HER verbal skills?

18. *Reliability:*
    a) Does S/HE attend appointments/work on time?
    b) Is S/HE prepared for meetings/work?
    c) Is S/HE trustworthy?
    d) Have you noticed any irregularities in HIS/HER behavior?

19. *Did you ever disagree about something with PERSON?*
    About what? How was it resolved?

20. *What one thing most impresses you about PERSON?*

21. *Would you re-hire PERSON?*

22. *Is there anything else that you think I should know in considering PERSON for this position?*

23. *Thank you very much for your time. Your input helps in the evaluation of the candidates.*

Appendix E: References

Darmohray, Tina, ed. *Job Descriptions for System Administrators.* 2d ed. Berkeley, Calif.: USENIX Association, 1997.

Swann, William S., Phillip Margulies, Masine Rasaler, and Hilary S. Kayle. *Swan's How to Pick the Right People Program.* New York: John Wiley & Sons, 1989.

Yate, Martin. *Hiring the Best: A Manager's Guide to Effective Interviewing*. 4th ed. Holbrook, Mass.: Bob Adams, Inc., 1994.